SCANDINAVIAN MYTHOLOGY

JASON PORTERFIELD

New York

Published in 2008 by The Rosen Publishing Group, Inc.
29 East 21st Street, New York, NY 10010

First Edition

Library of Congress Cataloging-in-Publication Data

Porterfield, Jason.
Scandinavian Mythology / Jason Porterfield.—1st ed.
    p. cm.—(Mythology around the world)
ISBN-13: 978-1-4042-0740-0
ISBN-10: 1-4042-0740-6
1. Mythology, Norse.
I. Title. II. Series.
BL860.P57 2006
293'.13—c22

                                                        2005037508

Manufactured in the United States of America

On the cover: A page from a tenth-century illuminated manuscript depicts a Norse longship with a dragon prow.

CONTENTS

INTRODUCTION

The Norse lived in Scandinavia, consisting of present-day Norway, Sweden, Finland, Denmark, and Iceland. Scandinavia was a formidable land of rugged mountains and Arctic tundra, icy fjords, and stony islands. The summer growing season was short, while winter seemed a cold and dark eternity. Norse culture was dominated by a warrior class called the Vikings. These seafaring men traded and raided along the coasts of Europe between 780 and 1070 CE. The characteristics most valued by the Norse—hardiness, bravery, loyalty, strength, and cunning—were also those that enabled them to survive the rigors of daily life on both land and sea.

The Norse mythological world was inspired by the drastic geography of the Scandinavian physical world. The dominant features of Scandinavia's landscape were transformed into mythological mountains, rivers, plains, and a vast sea. The volcanoes and glaciers of Iceland inspired the fiery realm of Muspell and the cold, shadowy world of Niflheim. Asgard, the world of the gods, resembled Scandinavia's fertile southern plains. Giants and dwarves inhabited mountainous worlds.

Norse mythology provided its believers with a framework through which to view their existence. They believed that the world was created from ice and fire, and that one day it would come to an end. They also concluded that it would be reborn, just

This map shows Europe in the sixteenth century. Though the Viking age had passed by the time that this map was drawn, Viking explorers' knowledge of Europe's coasts continued to influence mapmakers throughout the Renaissance period and beyond.

as spring eventually followed every long winter. In a land dominated by cold winters and dark days, they told tales of gods who were often unfair and fickle. This fatalism shows through in many of the myths in which gods cheat, steal, and kill.

The rugged landscape of Scandinavia made it difficult to farm in some areas. Many Scandinavians chose to take their chances at sea instead, by raiding coastal villages or establishing settlements elsewhere.

The gods themselves caused natural phenomena such as thunder and earthquakes, as well as embodied traits admired by the Vikings such as wisdom, cunning, fertility, and strength. Mythical humans like Sigurd offered an ideal toward which warriors could strive, while legendary kings ruled with justice and wisdom. By following

the examples of humans who refused to be daunted by the impulsive actions of the gods, the Norse could gain the respect and admiration of their peers. More important, noble acts in life could lead to a glorious afterlife of fighting and feasting in Valhalla—the hall of Odin—before standing beside the gods at the final battle of Ragnarok.

1 ANCIENT SCANDINAVIAN CULTURE

The Scandinavian culture originally developed from Germanic tribes—specifically a group called the Boat-Axe—who mostly lived around coastal Norway and southern Finland and Sweden, beginning around 2000 BCE. The Scandinavian Bronze Age, which lasted from about 1600 to 450 BCE, saw enormous advances in art and craftsmanship in fields such as shipbuilding and metalworking.

Several hundred years after the Bronze Age, Germanic tribes first began moving farther westward and northward during what is known as the Migration Period. By the end of this period, which lasted roughly from 300 to 900 CE, small kingdoms had been established across Scandinavia. The northern European settlers came to be called Norse.

Many Scandinavian carvers were highly skilled artisans, respected for their ability to render mythological figures from wood or stone. This sculpture from circa 1000 CE depicts a Viking warrior.

As Scandinavia became more heavily populated, greater numbers of people took to the sea to seek their fortunes. They were called Vikings, meaning "fighting men" or "bay men" in either Old English or Old Norse (the origins of the word "Viking" are somewhat unclear). The Vikings eventually spread throughout much of Europe, raiding coastal areas and establishing colonies. To the south, they colonized Scotland, Ireland, and parts of England; settled in parts of France; raided in Spain and Italy; and even established settlements on Sicily. Journeying east from the Baltic Sea, they navigated overland and by river to the Black Sea, reaching Kiev, now in present-day Ukraine; Constantinople, Turkey; and as far away as Baghdad, in present-day Iraq. Vikings sailing to the west colonized Iceland during the ninth and tenth centuries and established settlements in Greenland and North America.

The seafaring Vikings were fierce and adventurous, exploring and plundering distant parts of the world. They greatly admired individuals who were brave in battle and loyal to their leaders, friends, and family.

Life in Scandinavia

The Viking warriors and sailors represented only one side of the Scandinavian people. In Scandinavia, most people led peaceful lives. They lived by hunting, fishing, and farming, activities in which the Viking sailors also took part when they returned home from raiding and exploring.

The Vikings terrorized European coastlines in longships similar to the one shown in this wood carving. Swift, streamlined, and highly maneuverable, the longships were ideal for use in Norse raids.

The Scandinavians adhered to a rigid social order in which people were either serfs or free. Serfs endured miserable lives as nearly slaves, sharing tiny huts built of timber, sod, and clay with whatever animals they possessed. They were manual laborers, compelled to do the bidding of the upper classes without opportunity to better

their lot in life. Within the class of the free there were various tiers, with warriors, earls, and kings at the top. Most Scandinavians belonged to the peasant class and were smallholders—farmers who owned small tracts of land—or freemen, people who were at liberty to make their living as they chose. The freemen were farmers, artisans, and craftsmen.

The skalds were well-respected members of Scandinavian society. Large crowds often welcomed them to villages. Because of their prestige, they were sometimes invited to stay with the local nobility.

The earls and warriors of the upper classes were the wealthiest and most powerful members of society. With respect to Scandinavia, this wealth was counted in terms of ships, treasure, followers, and estates that would pass from eldest son to eldest son. During the winter, the warriors remained at home, attending to their estates, feasting, and making repairs to weapons, ships, and equipment. With the arrival of spring, they would again set out on voyages of plunder, trade, and exploration.

The Role of the Poets

Scandinavians did not leave an extensive written record. They did have a written language consisting of runes, a type of alphabet, which were carved into wood or stone. The carving was a long and difficult process and therefore not very practical for record keeping.

Instead, most records and histories were kept by poets called skalds, who made their living through composing verse. The Norse poets were held in very high esteem because they possessed the ability to remember and pass on the culture's history through verse. The poets and storytellers could easily recite poems and weave tales detailing the exploits of their greatest warriors, or those of the Norse gods themselves. The skalds traveled from country to country and were frequent guests in the courts of kings and nobles. Their recitals always drew crowds, and they were often richly rewarded with gold or jewels for their performances. Becoming a skald required an ability to commit long, complex poems to memory, as well as a quick mind capable of creating verses on the spot. Skalds often trained for years under the tutelage of older poets before performing on their own.

2 ORIGINS AND EVOLUTION OF SCANDINAVIAN MYTHOLOGY

Norse myths were once the substance of the dominant religion of Scandinavia, from the time that the Germanic tribes moved into the region to the introduction of Christianity. In Iceland, this happened in 1000 CE. Sweden was the last Scandinavian country to officially convert, around 1070. Even then, the old beliefs held on for a few more centuries. Myths explained the creation of the world and the reasons for natural phenomena like the transition from day to night or the cause of thunder and lightning. Some aspects of Scandinavian mythology, such as the idea of a great flood at the creation of the world and a fiery cataclysm at its end, are common in mythologies around the world.

The basis for Norse mythology began taking shape in Germanic Europe around 1000 BCE. There are many examples of parallels between the myths of those two regions. For example, the god Odin appeared in Germany as Wodan and in England as Woden.

The Texts of Scandinavian Mythology

The earliest written record of Germanic religion dates to the Roman historian Cornelius Tacitus (ca. 56–120 CE) and his book *Germania*, written during the first century. Most of the sources documenting Norse mythology were composed in Iceland in the thirteenth century, when the old religion had been displaced by Christianity. They were recorded by a few individuals interested in preserving them for future generations so that they wouldn't be forgotten following the transition to Christianity.

The earliest surviving Scandinavian poems are the skaldic poems, which contain much of the information we now have about the gods and goddesses worshipped by the Vikings. These verses, rich in metaphor and description, form the basis for many later mythological works.

Cornelius Tacitus was a Roman historian. In addition to writing *Germania*, a book describing the Germanic tribes, he is famous for recording the history of the Roman Empire and its rulers in *Histories* and *Annals*, which were written in the first century CE.

Straightforward narrations of various myths are called the Eddic poems. The *Poetic Edda* is a book with twenty-nine mythical and heroic poems. Besides the ones in this book, there are a few others of the same type, also called Eddic. The *Prose Edda*, written around 1220 by the Icelandic poet, scholar, and statesman Snorri Sturluson (1179–1241), drew extensively from the skaldic poems. Sturluson hoped to encourage his countrymen to compose verse in the skaldic

Many of the Icelandic Eddas were colorful and ornate. This eighteenth-century cover of the *Prose Edda* shows several figures from Scandinavian mythology, including Odin, Heimdall, Sleipnir, and Fenrir the wolf.

style, a complex form of poetry known for ornate wordplay and vivid imagery. His other major work, the *Heimskringla*, surveys Norwegian history from legendary times to the present. The Danish writer Saxo Grammaticus (ca. 1150–ca. 1216) recorded the myths and religious practices of Denmark and western Scandinavia in his work *Gesta Danorum*, written around 1215.

The Icelandic sagas also offer information about old Scandinavian religion. They were written in the thirteenth century by many poets and cover many subjects ranging from the lives of kings and heroes to tales of exploration and the histories of distinguished Icelandic families.

Centers of Faith

Archaeologists have discovered much information about Norse religious practices through excavations across Scandinavia. They've found that the development of Scandinavian religion can be traced to its sources in Norway, Sweden, and Denmark. Because Iceland was not colonized until the ninth century, the original Scandinavian countries give a sense of the sorts of places where the gods were worshipped.

Unlike most of the dominant religions today in which one god is worshipped, Norse society worshipped multiple gods. Rock carvings, standing stones covered in runes, and relics found in tombs provide insight into how the gods were imagined by their worshippers. Burial mounds were often stocked with weapons, food, useful items such as tools and clothing, and objects representing the gods and goddesses.

Picture stones, which are also called rune stones, such as this one from around the eleventh century, still stand throughout Scandinavia. These stones tell stories from Scandinavian mythology through runes and images. The myth depicted here involves Odin and a Goth named Ermaneric.

These objects were intended to help the individual in the afterlife. Particularly wealthy and powerful people were sometimes even buried with their boats.

In cities and towns throughout Scandinavia, temples decorated with larger-than-life statues of the gods provided places for the public to worship and to make sacrifices to the gods of their choice. In more rural areas, sacrifices were carried out on stone altars, usually located in high places such as hilltops or in groves. The gods were generally satisfied with animal sacrifices, but humans were occasionally sacrificed as well. The largest and most famous of the Norse temples was in Uppsala, where the streets were said to run red with blood from sacrifices. It is said to have been decorated with statues of the gods.

Scandinavians took their religion everywhere they traveled and continued to worship their gods while on journeys. However, they had little interest in spreading their religion and winning converts. Even when they colonized a location, they allowed locals to continue practicing their chosen religions.

3 THE SCANDINAVIAN MYTHOLOGICAL LANDSCAPE

According to Scandinavian myths, the world began with the meeting of ice and flame. From that moment, cascading events led to the creation of the gods, the various worlds, the sun, the moon, natural phenomena, and the races of humans, giants, elves, and dwarves.

The Giant Ymir and the Making of the World

At the beginning of time before the world was formed, there was a great void called Ginnungagap. Located to the south of the mighty gap was the Realm of Muspell, where eternal flames flickered. North of Ginnungagap, where frost and snow covered the realm called Niflheim, it was icy and cold. Eleven rivers, which originated from a spring called Hvergelmir, flowed from Niflheim. The rivers of Niflheim streamed into Ginnungagap, filling the northern half with frost, and hot air from Muspell blew up into Ginnungagap from the south. The cold and the heat met in the middle, where the warm breeze melted the cold frost. Life emerged from the liquid produced by the melting ice.

The first being created from this liquid was an evil frost giant named Ymir. While he slept, a race of giants sprang from his legs.

In this image, Thor meets the giant Ymir, whose body was used by Odin as raw materials for creating the world.

More ice melted, and next a cow called Audumla formed from those drops. Audumla's milk fed Ymir, and she got her nourishment by licking ice. As Audumla licked, a man named Buri gradually emerged from a block of ice. Buri's son Bor married a frost giant named Bestla and had three sons, Odin, Vili, and Ve.

These three sons hated the cruel giant Ymir and the other frost giants. Eventually, they killed Ymir. He bled so much that all but two of the frost giants drowned in his blood. The two survivors, Bergelmir and his wife, floated to safety on a boat made from a hollow tree.

Odin, Vili, and Ve carried Ymir's remains to the center of Ginnungagap and made the world from his body. His flesh became the earth while his unbroken bones formed mountains. They used his teeth, jaws, and broken bones to make boulders, rocks, and stones. They ringed Earth with a wide sea made from his blood. They created the sky from his skull and placed a dwarf under each of the four corners, naming them North, South, East, and West. They took sparks and embers from Muspell and placed them high in Ginnungagap, forming the sun, the moon, and the stars.

The three brothers marked off tracts of land at the edge of Earth and gave them to the giants. This land became the realm of Jotunheim. The giants settled there but were so hostile that the three brothers were forced to use one of Ymir's eyebrows to enclose a vast portion of Earth. They called this area Midgard. They made the first man and woman on Earth, named Ask and Embla, from two fallen trees, an ash and an elm. They lived in Midgard, and all people are descended from them. The brothers also gave the maggots, which swarmed Ymir's body, the shape and intelligence of humans. The maggots became dwarves who lived underground.

The natural cycles of night and day came about after the giant Narvi gave birth to a daughter with black hair, black eyes, and a dark complexion, named Night. Night had a son named Day whose fair hair and complexion were dazzling. Odin took Night and Day and placed each in separate horse-drawn chariots and set them in the sky to journey across it at half-day intervals. At the same time, a man in Midgard named Mundilfari had two beautiful children, a son named Moon and a daughter called Sun. Odin and the other gods placed the children in the sky to guide the chariots, which draw the moon and sun across the sky. Sun is pursued by the wolf Skoll, whose brother Hati chases the moon.

After Earth was finished and populated by humans, giants, and dwarves, the gods created Asgard, a green land with many towering palaces. They built a flaming rainbow bridge called Bifrost, which meant "trembling roadway," to link Asgard with Midgard. The Aesir, who were warrior gods, then crossed Bifrost and settled in Asgard, with Odin reigning over them as the oldest and greatest of the gods.

The Nine Worlds

The world that sprang out of Ginnungagap and Ymir's body actually consisted of a roughly three-tiered cosmos made up of nine worlds: Asgard, Vanaheim, Alfheim, Midgard, Jotunheim, Nidavellir,

The giant ash tree Yggdrasill passes through every world, sustaining life. This illustration shows the three main worlds and the many animals and monsters that live off of Yggdrasill.

Svartalfheim, Niflheim, and Hel. A large pantheon of gods and goddesses shared it with humans, giants, elves, dwarves, and magical creatures.

The universe consisted of three tiers stacked on top of each other like plates. A great wall built by a giant surrounded Asgard, situated on the top tier. The Aesir lived in Asgard. Every day they gathered at the magical Well of Urd, located on the plain of Gladsheim. Three goddesses called the Norns presided over the well. Their names were Urd (Fate), Skuld (Being), and Verdandi (Necessity). They controlled the destiny of every human.

The great hall of Valhalla, the hall of the Einherjar (Honored Dead), was located in Asgard. Valkyries, female warriors who rode winged horses, carried these warriors to Valhalla after they died in battle. There, the Einherjar awaited Ragnarok, the great battle that occurs at the end of time and destroys the world. They spend eternity fighting all day and feasting with Odin every night.

The upper level also included the realms of Vanaheim and Alfheim. Fertility gods called the Vanir lived in Vanaheim until they joined the Aesir in Asgard. Alfheim was home to the light elves, who generally play little part in the surviving myths.

Midgard, the realm of humans, was located on the second level and was surrounded by a vast ocean. The great serpent Jormungand, who was so large that he had to swallow his tail, lived on the bottom of the ocean. The giants' realm, Jotunheim, lay either in the mountainous eastern part of Midgard or across the ocean, depending on the myth. Their fortress, Utgard, stood at the center of

Jotunheim. To the north, the dwarves lived in caves and potholes in a land called Nidavellir (Dark Fields). A race called the dark elves, who are interchangeable with the dwarves within the myths, lived somewhere below Midgard in Svartalfheim (Land of the Dark Elves). The rainbow bridge Bifrost connected Midgard to Asgard, and the Iving River, which never froze, separated Jotunheim from Asgard.

The third level was home to Niflheim, the world of the dead. Niflheim was a world of cold and darkness. Its citadel was a place of high walls and forbidding gates called Hel, where those who died in accidents and of old age were doomed to eternity. In some sources, Niflheim and Hel constitute only one world, rather than two. The land of fire, Muspell, was the ninth world.

Yggdrasill

Yggdrasill, a mighty ash tree, served as an axis for all of the nine worlds. Yggdrasill stood when the world was created, survived the end-of-the-world battle Ragnarok, and was still alive during the rebirth of the world that followed. Norse mythology offers no explanation for the tree's presence. It has simply existed since the beginning of time and continues to exist after the end of the world.

Yggdrasill has three roots. One root is in Asgard, under the Well of Urd. A second root taps into Jotunheim at the Spring of Mimir, whose water brings wisdom to those who drink it. The third root is in Niflheim. The Spring of Hvergelmir flows from under this root.

Yggdrasill guards and protects all life, and it is associated with a number of mythical animals. The dragon Nidhogg and other serpents gnaw on the root located in Hel. Deer and goats leap along the branches and feed on leaves and new growth. An eagle named Vidofnir perches in its uppermost branches, and the squirrel Ratatosk scurries up and down the trunk carrying insults back and forth between Nighogg and the eagle. When Ragnarok comes, a man named Lif and a woman named Lifthrasir hide inside Yggdrasill's trunk. There, they survive the world's destruction by fire and flood and make a new beginning for humanity when the world is re-created.

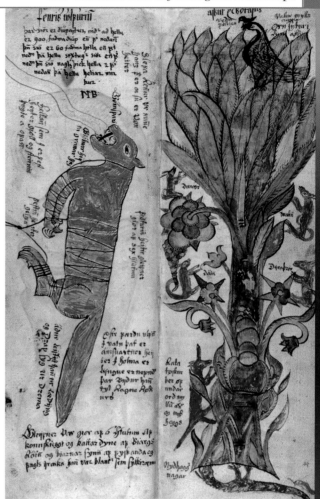

This page from an Icelandic illuminated manuscript shows the wolf Fenrir *(left)* and Yggdrasill *(right)*. According to Norse mythology, Fenrir is one of Loki's monstrous children who will take part in the world's destruction at the battle of Ragnarok. Afterward, Yggdrasill remains standing, continuing to support life.

4 THE SCANDINAVIAN GODS AND GODDESSES

The gods and heroes of Scandinavian mythology singularly represent both the best and the worst of human nature. They are strong and knowledgeable, and they stand to preserve order against a chaos represented by giants and monsters. Many, like Thor, represent a heroic ideal for humans to aspire toward. However, the gods are also flawed and sometimes give in to greed or anger. The gods can be very human as well as very divine.

The gods and goddesses initially existed as two separate groups: the Aesir and the Vanir. The Aesir were the warrior gods, while the Vanir were fertility gods. In all, there were twelve gods and thirteen goddesses.

This sculpture depicts Odin sitting on his throne, Hlidskjalf, and supporting his spear, Gungnir, with his left hand. The ravens Huginn and Muninn are perched on Odin's shoulders.

The War Between the Aesir and the Vanir

The Aesir and the Vanir initiated the world's first war, which began when Aesir killed a witch named Gullveig because of her greed. The Vanir were angered by this and swore vengeance against the Aesir. They prepared for war.

The Aesir soon found out that the Vanir planned to attack and so they gathered their strength for battle. Odin then got involved and cast his enchanted spear, Gungnir, into the gathering of Vanir. The two groups fought back and forth, destroying large portions of their respective realms. Eventually, it became clear that neither side could win and they met to discuss a truce. They agreed to live side by side in harmony and exchanged leaders as a gesture of goodwill. Njord, Freyr, Freya, and Kvasir of the Vanir went to live in Asgard. Honir and Mimir moved to Vanaheim.

Odin and Thor

Odin was the leader of the Aesir. The oldest and wisest of all of the gods, he made significant sacrifices in his pursuit of knowledge. He visited the spring of Mimir, where he sacrificed an eye to win the right to drink its water. With this drink he gained both insight and the desire for more knowledge. Odin learned nine songs of power from the wise giant Bolthor. He learned eighteen magic runes, which brought him vast powers. He raised seeresses and sorcerers from the dead in order to learn their secrets. Most drastically, he hanged himself from one of Yggdrasill's branches in order to gain occult wisdom, then returned to life with the ability to use it in the living world.

Odin was known as Allfather for his age, power, and role in the creation of the world. He was the god of war, poetry, and wisdom. He was also the patron god of the Scandinavian upper class, as well as of the poets and storytellers. Of the gods, a majority were Odin's sons.

Wherever Odin went, he wore a blue cloak and carried a magical spear called Gungnir. His golden arm ring, Draupnir, was also magical, and eight new rings dropped from it every nine days. Draupnir was a symbol for renewal. He often disguised his fierce appearance by wearing a broad-brimmed hat pulled low over his missing eye and changed his shape at will. Two ravens named Huginn ("Thought" in Old Norse) and Muninn ("Memory," also in Old Norse) sat on his shoulders. The birds symbolized both Odin's warlike nature and his quest for wisdom. His horse, Sleipnir, had eight legs and was capable of outrunning any other horse alive and bearing its rider to the land of the dead and back again. Odin could see all that happened in the nine worlds from his high throne, Hlidskjalf, in Asgard.

Odin's son Thor was second in the Norse pantheon. From the descriptions handed down by the Eddic poets and saga writers, he was the most popular and respected of the gods. The farming peasantry and freemen, who made up most of the Scandinavian population, worshipped Thor. Odin represented war, while Thor stood for order. His name was invoked when people desired law and stability.

In this painting, Thor brings thunder and lightning to battle with him as he swings his hammer, Mjollnir, against the giants. Thor's chariot is pulled by a team of goats.

Physically, Thor epitomized the ideal Viking warrior. He was huge and enormously strong, with a large red beard and a vast appetite. Thor lost his temper quickly, but he regained it just as quickly. Though he was not very clever, Thor was always dependable and trustworthy. He used his magical war hammer, Mjollnir, to fight giants and trolls.

Thor was the god of thunder, which was caused by the sound of his chariot rolling across the ground. His hammer, Mjollnir, caused lightning. Scandinavians believed that violent storms with heavy rains and high winds were a sign of Thor's anger, but they also could call on him for the helpful rain that made the crops grow.

Other Principal Gods

Njord, chief among the Vanir, was god of the sea and winds. Of the gods, Njord was the only one who did not eventually live in Asgard. Instead, he reigned in a palace under the sea. His son, Freyr, was a fertility god. Freyr decided when the sun would shine and also had some control over the weather. Among his possessions were a magical ship called *Skidbladnir* and a boar with golden bristles.

The gods Tyr, Balder, Hod, Bragi, Ull, Vali, and Vidar were Odin's sons. Tyr was the bravest of the Aesir. He sacrificed a hand so that the evil wolf Fenrir could be captured and bound until Ragnarok. Balder was the most gentle and beautiful of the Aesir. His brother Hod was blind. Forseti, Balder's son, was the god of justice.

Bragi was god of eloquence and public speaking. He was regarded as the best poet among the gods, even though Odin was the god of poetry. Ull was god of archery and skiing. Participants in duels invoked Ull for protection. Vali and Vidar were extremely young gods, renowned for their immunity to fire and water.

Heimdall, who is sometimes described as Odin's son, had nine mothers—the waves of the ocean. Because he needed little sleep and had the sharpest senses, he was the guardian and watchman of the gods. Heimdall's horn, Gjoll, could be heard throughout the nine worlds, and Heimdall blew it to assemble the gods in times of trouble.

Honir was an indecisive figure who shared several adventures with Odin and Loki and was raised as Odin's foster brother. Along with the unfortunate Mimir, he went to live with the Vanir after the war between the gods ended. Honir eventually moved back to Asgard.

The deaths of two of the lesser gods served to benefit Odin. Mimir, the wisest of the Aesir, had his head cut off by the Vanir after the war between the gods ended. Odin preserved Mimir's head, which was still capable of speech, and gained a great deal of knowledge by consulting it. Kvasir, the wisest of the Vanir, was killed by a pair of dwarves who mixed his blood with honey to make a potent mead called the Mead of Poetry. A giant killed them, and Odin obtained it from the daughter of that giant.

Loki

Loki, the handsome and charming god of mischief, was the son of two giants. Extremely cunning and sharp-tongued, he often put the gods into difficult situations and then had to use his wits to return

The other gods eventually tire of Loki's tricks and chain him to a rock, where his loyal wife, Sigyn, tries to shield him from the serpent's burning venom by catching it in a bowl.

things to normal. Loki was also capable of changing his shape and sex, and he often used this shape-shifting ability to cause trouble.

Loki was the father of three dangerous monsters: the serpent Jormungand, the wolf Fenrir, and the ghoulish figure Hel, who reigned over the domain of the same name. Loki's mischief was usually playful. However, as time passed, his dissatisfaction with the rest of the gods grew and he began acting out of malice. The gods eventually bound him for the trouble he caused. Afterward, he caused earthquakes by thrashing in his fetters.

Freya and the Norse Goddesses

Less is known of the Norse goddesses than of the gods, since much of the information about their characters has been lost over time. Many sources cite their equality with the gods. Of the goddesses, the most complete figure was Freya, the goddess of love. She was Njord's daughter and Freyr's sister. Beautiful and adventurous, she was also associated with battle and is described as riding a war chariot pulled by two cats. Some myths claim that she divided the spirits of those killed in battle with Odin, taking her half to her hall at Sessrumnir, while the other half went to Valhalla to fight and feast with the Allfather.

A skilled sorceress, she was sometimes known as the goddess of magic. During a trip to Niflheim, Freya gained a power to know destinies. She owned an enchanted falcon skin, which allowed her to change into a bird. Her other prized possession, a gorgeous, dwarf-forged necklace called the Necklace of the Brisings, represented her role as a fertility goddess.

Far less is known of the other principal goddesses. Gefjon had a special connection with unmarried women. Eir was the goddess of healing who was either invoked in illness or after an injury. Sjöfn and Lofn inspired love between humans, while Var listened when the marriage oath was pledged and punished those who broke their wedding vows.

The goddess Frigg, who was Odin's wife and Balder's mother, watched over women in labor and knew people's destinies.

5 HEROES AND VILLAINS IN SCANDINAVIAN MYTHOLOGY

Most of the surviving texts from Norse mythology tell stories about the gods and goddesses, with dwarves and giants also playing significant roles. However, a few tales do exist detailing the exploits of humans who had special relationships with members of the Norse pantheon. Death and hardship as dealt out by the gods were something to be endured or even mocked.

The Ransom of Otter

One day, as Odin, Honir, and Loki journeyed through Midgard, they came upon an otter catching a salmon. Clever Loki killed the otter with a stone. The gods traveled on until they came to a farmhouse, where they asked to stay the night. The gods showed the farmer, Hreidmar, the otter and salmon as evidence that they could provide the night's meal. The otter was actually Hreidmar's son, Otter, who took animal form while fishing.

That night, Hreidmar and Otter's brothers, Fafnir and Regin, surprised the sleeping gods and bound them. When Odin learned the truth about Otter, he offered to pay a ransom to Hreidmar. Hreidmar agreed to let the gods go if they covered Otter's skin with gold. Loki then set off for the gold while the others remained behind.

To get the gold, Loki captured and threatened the dwarf Andvari, who turned over all of his gold in two sacks. Loki, however, noticed that Andvari had kept one golden ring for himself. He threatened the dwarf again, who put a curse on the ring as he handed it over. Putting it on his own finger, Loki left for Hreidmar's farm.

When Loki returned, he gave the ring to Odin and the three gods piled gold over Otter's skin. Hreidmar inspected their work and found a whisker showing. Odin placed the ring over the whisker. After the gods were freed, Loki warned the farmer and his sons that the ring was cursed and the curse would pass to them. With that, they left Hreidmar and his sons to their fate.

Sigurd the Giant Slayer

The story of Andvari's cursed ring continues in the tale of Sigurd the Giant Slayer, the greatest Norse hero. Sigurd's father was Sigmund, the son of King Volsung. On the night of Sigmund's twin sister, Signy's, wedding feast, a mysterious one-eyed stranger wearing a broad-brimmed hat entered the hall. He thrust a magnificent sword into Branstock, the tree that supported Volsung's hall, and announced that it belonged to anyone who could draw it from the tree. The stranger said that the great sword would never fail until the day he called the owner to him. Every Viking at the gathering tugged at the sword, but nobody could budge it until Sigmund easily pulled it out of the tree.

As the stranger promised, it served Sigmund well for years. One day, as Sigmund and his men faced King Volsung's murderer, King

This piece of armor, found in a seventh-century boat grave in Uppsala, Sweden, is called Sigurd's Helmet, after the Sigurd myth.

Siggeir, in combat, the one-eyed stranger appeared on the battlefield. Sigmund swung at him with his sword, but the stranger deflected the blow with a mighty spear and broke the sword into three pieces. Sigmund later died of his wounds. Sigmund's wife, Hiordis, fled to Denmark, where she gave birth to Sigurd.

When he was old enough, Sigurd's stepfather, Alf, apprenticed him to Hreidmar's son Regin, who was a highly skilled blacksmith. Years before, Regin's brother Fafnir had killed their father for treasure and turned himself into a dragon. The crafty Regin schemed to possess the treasure for himself. He persuaded Sigurd to allow him to reforge Sigmund's great sword, and sent the boy to face Fafnir.

On his journey to Fafnir's lair, Sigurd met a one-eyed stranger that he recognized as Odin. The stranger advised him that to avoid being scorched by the dragon's flames, he must dig a pit in the dragon's path and stab him from beneath.

Sigurd followed Odin's counsel and slew Fafnir. Regin then asked Sigurd to cook the dragon's heart for him. Sigurd burnt his thumb while roasting the dragon's heart. He put his scorched thumb in his mouth, and suddenly, he could understand the speech of birds. He heard two nuthatches discussing Regin's plot to kill Sigurd and seize the treasure for himself. He turned around just as Regin raised his dagger to strike, and Sigurd beheaded Regin with one stroke of his sword. Sigurd then took Andvari's ring from the dragon's hoard and put it on his finger.

Upon hearing the nuthatches talking about a beautiful maiden in Hindfell, Sigurd rode there to find her. His horse Grani—descendant of Odin's own horse, Sleipner—leapt through a barrier of magical flames into a castle courtyard at Hindfell. There, he rescued the beautiful Brynhild. One of Odin's Valkyries, Brynhild was put into an enchanted sleep for disobeying Odin's orders. She had sworn to Odin that she would wed the first human she met upon waking. Sigurd and Brynhild declared their love for each other, and Sigurd gave Brynhild the gold ring.

The cursed ring brought doom to both, however. Despite Brynhild's oath, they were tricked into marrying other people. One day, the brothers of Brynhild's other husband ambushed and killed Sigurd. Brynhild threw herself onto Sigurd's blazing funeral pyre, and together they ascended to Valhalla.

Dwarves

Dwarves such as Andvari frequently played a role in the myths of Norse gods. They are usually portrayed as villains because of their greed and selfishness. The dwarves were excellent smiths and craftsmen, though, and they created many of the objects treasured by the gods. Two dwarves called the Sons of Ivaldi spun from gold the hair of Sif, Thor's wife, after Loki cut off her real hair as a joke. The dwarves also made Odin's spear, Gungnir, and Freyr's ship, *Skidbladnir*, which could be folded up and carried in his pocket.

When Loki carried the hair, the spear, and the ship from Nidavellir to Asgard, he bet two dwarves, Brokk and Eitri, that they couldn't meet the quality of the craftsmanship of the goods he was carrying. The dwarves met the challenge by forging Odin's magic arm ring, Draupnir; Thor's war hammer, Mjollnir; and Freyr's boar

The gods valued the craftsmanship of the dwarves and had many interactions with them. Here, Freya, the goddess of love and beauty, is shown visiting the dwarves who are making her Necklace of the Brisings.

with golden bristles. When they brought these wonders to Asgard, the gods declared Brokk and Eitri the winners. The dwarves demanded Loki's head as their price. Loki agreed, but he refused to let them touch any part of his neck. Since they couldn't cut off his head without touching the neck, they compromised and sewed Loki's lips together.

The Giant Hrungnir

The gods were constantly at war with the giants. In many ways the mirror opposites of the gods, the giants wished to overturn the order of Asgard and throw the world into chaos.

Hrungnir was widely considered the strongest of the giants. One day, Odin himself confronted Hrungnir. He rode Sleipnir into Jotunheim, right to the mighty giant's palace. Hrungnir, impressed by Sleipnir's speed but not realizing the rider was Odin, suggested they stage a race with his own horse, Gold Mane. Odin led the giant into Asgard, where he invited him into Valhalla to drink.

The giant quickly became drunk and began insulting the gods. Odin soon regretted the invitation and called for Thor. The giant promptly challenged Thor to a duel on the border between Jotunheim and Asgard. Thor killed Hrungnir, but he was pinned to the ground by the giant's leg. None of the gods could free him until Thor's young son Magni lifted the leg. In return, Thor gave his son the horse Gold Mane.

Kings of History and Legend

The Yngling kings ruled Sweden from the city of Uppsala around the fifth and sixth centuries. According to the legend, Freyr himself had ruled Sweden from the city during a time of great prosperity. The human kings who ruled after him took his name, calling themselves the Ynglings after Yngvi-Freyr.

When Freyr died, he was placed under a great burial mound by the people of the royal court and his death was concealed from the people. His courtiers brought offerings of gold, silver, and copper and placed them in three holes in the mound. (Upon death, nobles were often buried in mounds along with treasures and goods for the afterlife.) After three years, the people finally learned that Freyr was

In this illustration from a fourteenth-century manuscript of the *Prose Edda*, a disguised King Gylfi, the legenary Swedish king, questions Odin about the origins of the world.

dead. When the truth came out, the people decided that since the seasons had continued to bring plentiful harvests, Freyr must have still been helping them. They named him god of the earth.

The legendary King Gylfi, who ruled Sweden in the time before the Yngling kings, did not come off as well in his brush with the gods. Once Odin sent the goddess Gefion to Midgard to find land. She met King Gylfi, who offered her as much land as she could plow. She changed her four giant sons into oxen and plowed all around a large swath of land. The oxen completely separated it from Sweden, and it drifted out to sea. Today it is the island of Zealand, site of the present-day city of Copenhagen in Denmark.

6 THE SCANDINAVIAN MYTHS

Scandinavian myths reveal many sides to the gods. Some show them as noble, while others present them as scheming and deceitful. Their adventures, both comic and tragic, range across the nine worlds from Asgard to Hel.

Asgard's Wall

After the war with the Vanir, the wall around Asgard lay in ruins. Nothing stood to protect the realm of the gods against invaders. Though the gods wanted the wall rebuilt, none of them was eager to invest time and energy into such a difficult task.

One day, a lone figure on horseback approached Asgard. Upon meeting Heimdall, the stranger declared that he had a plan to offer to the gods. Heimdall led him to Gladsheim, where the stranger offered to rebuild the wall around Asgard and make it even stronger than before in just eighteen months. When Odin asked the price, the stranger said that he wanted to marry Freya and to own the sun and moon. The gods were outraged. Odin initially refused, but Loki suggested that they take the offer and give the man only six months to build the wall, an impossible deadline. The man agreed on the condition that the gods allow his horse to help him. The gods saw no reason to refuse this request, and the deal was made.

This Norse carving from Gotland, Sweden, depicts warriors who were killed in battle marching to join Odin in Valhalla. Odin's horse, Sleipnir, carries one warrior, while those behind him walk with their swords pointed downward to signify death.

The man started work the next day. The gods were astonished to see how much stone he could lift and the horse could drag. As he began shaping it and setting it into place, it became obvious that the man was really a giant in disguise. The wall grew rapidly, and the gods became less certain they'd win the bargain.

In a panic, they became angry with Loki for striking the deal and made him swear to guarantee that the giant would lose the wager. Loki agreed, and the next day he turned himself into a mare. The giant's stallion ran off with the disguised trickster, and he was unable to haul any stone that day. The giant realized that without his horse, he would be unable to finish the wall on time. He flew into a giant rage. The gods then sent for Thor, who promptly killed the giant.

The Apples of Youth

One day, Loki, Odin, and Honir traveled to Midgard. As the day waned, they decided to make camp and find something to eat. Loki killed an ox and began roasting it over their fire. No matter how long they kept it over the flame, the meat would not cook. The three gods were growing impatient and hungry when they spotted an eagle sitting nearby. The eagle suggested that the meat would cook if they allowed it to eat some of the meat, too. They agreed, and the meat cooked quickly. When they offered it to the eagle, the bird took the largest and best pieces of meat and began to eat.

Furious, Loki struck the eagle with his staff. The staff lodged in the eagle's back, and the bird took flight. Loki was unable to let go and was carried into the air. Loki begged for mercy, and the eagle offered to let him go if he could bring Bragi's wife, Idun, and her apples out of Asgard. Idun's apples were said to prevent the effects of aging, and their presence in Asgard kept the gods young and vigorous. The gods are immortal only by the grace of Idun's apples. Loki, worried about his own plight, did not consider the consequences of the apples leaving Asgard. The eagle dropped Loki after he promised to lead Idun and her basket of apples over Bifrost.

On the appointed day, Loki convinced Idun that he had found a tree with golden apples on the other side of Bifrost. Loki persuaded Idun to go out with him to compare her apples with the others he said he had found. She agreed, and they set out. As soon as they entered Midgard, the eagle, who was really the giant Thiazi in disguise, swooped down and grabbed Idun and her apples before flying away.

The gods soon missed Idun, and without her apples they began aging rapidly. Alarmed, Odin called all of the gods together at the Well of Gladsheim, where it became clear that Heimdall had seen Loki leading Idun over Bifrost. The gods seized Loki and forced the truth from him. He agreed to return Idun and the apples to Asgard.

Borrowing Freya's falcon skin, Loki flew to Thiazi's home in Jotunheim, where he found Idun alone. He turned her into a nut and flew off with her clutched in his talons. When the giant returned and found Idun and the apples gone, he turned into an eagle and flew off in pursuit of Loki. He was closing in on the trickster when he flew into a wall of flame, which the gods had put around Asgard. His wings burning, the giant fell to the ground and was killed by the gods. Loki changed Idun back to her usual form, and she promptly offered her apples to the waiting gods.

The beloved god Balder falls, killed accidentally by a twig of mistletoe that was made into a dart and thrown by his blind brother, Hod. Loki is seen in the background after aiming the dart.

Balder's Death

Balder was the most beloved of the gods and goddesses living in Asgard. Therefore, the other gods became greatly concerned when he began having nightmares. Odin vowed to discover their meaning. Mounting his horse, Sleipnir, he rode down to Niflheim and into Hel, where he encountered many golden ornaments decorating the halls. Odin worked his magic spells and raised a dead seeress. Upon interrogation, the seeress revealed that Hel was expecting Balder's sudden death at the hands of his blind brother, Hod.

When he returned to Asgard with this terrible information, the gods gathered to determine the best way to protect Balder. They named everything in the world that could cause sudden death. Frigg, Balder's mother, then traveled throughout the nine worlds, asking each substance to swear an oath never to harm Balder. Animals, elements such as fire and water, iron, rocks, and every other imaginable thing swore not to harm him. Satisfied, Frigg returned to Asgard and told the gods what she had done. They promptly began testing the results by throwing different objects at Balder and striking him with weapons such as axes and arrows. None caused him harm, and the gods continued to amuse themselves with this new game.

Loki resented the fact that nothing could hurt Balder. He changed himself into an old woman and went to visit Frigg. In disguise, he asked her if she had truly gotten everything that existed to swear an oath not to harm Balder. Frigg answered that she had not asked the mistletoe, believing it to be too small and young to cause harm. Loki left, in search of mistletoe. He found a sprig and fashioned it into a dart.

When he returned to Asgard, the gods had patient Balder standing against a wall and were throwing darts at him. Loki noticed that Hod was not participating and approached the blind god. He gave the dart to Hod and offered to guide his hand when he threw. Hod, not knowing that the dart could hurt his brother, agreed. When the dart struck Balder, it passed all the way through him and he fell dead. The gods were stunned into silence, and Loki fled the scene. He changed shape many times, finally becoming a salmon in the river Frarnang, where the gods captured him using a net. Afterward, they chained him to a rock deep beneath the earth's surface. They placed a poisonous serpent above him, where its burning venom would constantly drip onto his head. Loki remained there until the battle of Ragnarok.

Ragnarok

The battle that heralds the end of the world begins with bloody wars throughout Midgard. An unending winter called Fimbulvetr settles over the world, covering all of the land with ice. The wolf Skoll captures and eats the sun, while the wolf Hati devours the moon. The stars disappear, mountains and trees collapse, and anything that was bound breaks free. Waves crash against the shore as the serpent Jormungand thrashes, and the giants prepare for battle. Loki, freed from his imprisonment, joins the giants along with his daughter, Hel, and his monstrous sons, Jormungand and the wolf Fenrir. All of the spirits of Hel join their army, as do the fire giants of Muspell, led by fearsome Surt.

The gods and goddesses, led by Odin and joined by the Einherjar from Valhalla, assemble on the plain of Vigrid to meet the giants and their army. When the two armies collide in battle, they virtually destroy each other. Fenrir eats Odin. Thor and Jormungund kill each other. Vidar avenges Odin by killing Fenrir. The giant Surt slays Freyr and then begins flinging fire in every direction.

The wolf Fenrir eats Odin at the battle of Ragnarok in this carving, known as the Andreas Stone. One of Odin's ravens is shown still perched on his shoulder.

Every living thing dies, and Earth sinks into the sea.

However, it rises again. Vidar and Vali survive the fire and flood, as do Thor's sons Modi and Magni, who inherit his war hammer, Mjollnir. Balder and Hod return from the dead. They journey to the green land of Idavoll where their halls once stood. There they meet Honir, who becomes their chief. The sons of Odin's brothers Vili and Ve also arrive, adding to the number of new gods. They remake the world as a better place. Finally, when everything is ready, Lif and Lifthrasir emerge from Yggdrasill's trunk to begin the human race anew.

7 THE SCANDINAVIAN LEGACY

Though it was the region's dominant religion for many centuries, Norse mythology began to fade from prominence as Christianity made its way to Scandinavia. The Vikings were not immune to influence from other religions. As they encountered Christians wearing the sign of the cross around their necks, some took to wearing a charm called the Hammer of Thor around their own. Though it normally hung from the bottom of the hammer's handle, it could be turned upside-down to resemble a cross when Viking ships entered Christian ports.

    For the most part, the transition to Christianity was a slow and sometimes painful process. The exception was in Iceland, where the population voted to reject the old ways in favor of Christianity around 1000 CE. The other Scandinavian countries formally converted to Christianity as the

After the introduction of Christianity to Scandinavia, religious charms such as this silver Hammer of Thor amulet—which could also be worn as a Christian cross— took on greater significance for many Scandinavians.

result of decisions taken by kings and the upper classes. In Sweden, Christian missionaries attempted to teach people that the gods were really demons sent by the devil, but the people could not see their beloved gods as evil. The old temples were destroyed, and churches were built in their place. Though some beliefs persisted, they were far from an organized system and mostly involved Odin, Thor, and Freya.

A few remnants of the old Scandinavian religion persist in daily life. The days of the week from Tuesday to Friday are named for some of the Scandinavian gods. Tuesday is Tyr's Day, Wednesday is Odin's (or Woden's) Day, Thursday is Thor's Day, and Friday is Frigg's Day.

Pre-Christian traditions linger in many of the holidays celebrated in Scandinavia. The Mid-Summer's Eve celebration takes place on the longest day of the year and includes singing and dancing around the maypole—an old Norse fertility symbol—and bonfires celebrating the sun's power over darkness. On Walpurgis Night, celebrated on the evening of April 30, bonfires are set to hurry the coming of summer and drive away evil. The Santa Lucia Festival, held during the darkest days of mid-December, involves the lighting of candles in a ritual to express faith that the sun will return. Many Scandinavian Christmas customs, such as costumes, decorations, songs, and dances, are remnants of the old Yule celebrations of pre-Christian Scandinavia. One of the most popular Scandinavian Christmas decorations is a straw goat named Julbock, which represents one of the goats that pulled Thor's chariot.

In Sweden, Walpurgis Night is still celebrated with bonfires, which were originally used to drive away wolves and evil spirits such as witches and demons. This festival, held on April 30, continues to signify the end of winter and the celebration of springtime.

The Myths in Music and Literature

In music, the German composer Richard Wagner (1813–1833) revived the myths and retold them in operatic form. His masterpiece, *Der Ring des Nibelungen*, is a cycle of four operas entitled *Das Rheingold*, *Die Walküre*, *Siegfreid*, and *Götterdämmerung*. The opera cycle tells the story of the magical ring forged by the dwarf Alberich (Andvari in Norse mythology) and the hero Siegfreid's (called Sigurd in the Norse myths) quest to acquire it.

The Norse myths have also influenced literature. The most notable example is J. R. R. Tolkein's *Lord of the Rings* trilogy, which drew figures such as dwarves, elves, and trolls from the mythology, as well as the story of a cursed ring. Many other writers working in the genres of fantasy and science fiction have also drawn on Norse mythology for inspiration. Whether they realize it or not, readers of these genres are often exposed to characters and themes from one of the world's most enduring mythological traditions.

GLOSSARY

Edda A collection of Norse poetry.

indigenous Originating and living naturally in a region or environment.

mead An alcoholic beverage made of fermented honey and water.

occult Of or relating to supernatural agencies, their effects, or knowledge of them.

pantheon The officially recognized gods of a religion considered as a group.

rune A character in any of the ancient Germanic alphabets used in Scandinavia from about the third to thirteenth centuries.

saga An Icelandic narrative recorded between the twelfth and fourteenth centuries that describes events of the historic and legendary past.

seeress A woman who can divine the future.

serf A member of the lowest social class who is bound to the land.

skald The courtly poet-musicians of the Viking age.

Valhalla The warrior's heaven in Norse mythology; also called the Hall of the Honored Dead.

Valkyrie A maiden warrior of Norse mythology.

FOR MORE INFORMATION

American-Scandinavian Foundation
Scandinavia House—The Nordic Center in America
58 Park Avenue
New York, NY 10016
(212) 879-9779
Web sites: http://www.amscan.org
   http://www.scandinavia.com/culture/world/new-york.htm
   http://www.scandinaviahouse.org

Joseph Campbell Foundation
P.O. Box 36
San Anselmo, CA 94979-0036
(800) 330-6984
Web site: http://www.jcf.org/index2.php

Museum of National Antiquities
Narvavägen 13-17
Stockholm, Sweden
Web site: http://www.historiska.se/home/

Northvegr Foundation
P.O. Box 174
Lapeer, MI 48446
Web site: http://www.northvegr.org/main.php

Project Runeberg
LYSATOR Academic Computer Society
Linköping University
Linköping, Sweden
Web site: http://runeberg.org

Web Sites

Due to the changing nature of Internet links, Rosen Publishing has developed an online list of Web sites related to the subject of this book. This site is updated regularly. Please use this link to access the list:

http://www.rosenlinks.com/maw/scan

FOR FURTHER READING

Ardagh, Philip. *Norse Myths & Legends*. Chicago, IL: World
    Book, 2002.

Berger, Gilda. *The Real Vikings: Craftsmen, Traders and Fearsome
    Raiders*. Washington, DC: National Geographic Children's
    Books, 2003.

Branston, Brian. *Gods and Heroes from the Viking Mythology*. New
    York, NY: Peter Bedrick Books, 1994.

Culom, Padraic. *The Children of Odin: The Book of Northern Myths*.
    New York, NY: Macmillan, 1984.

Daly, Kathleen N. *Norse Mythology A to Z: A Young Reader's
    Companion*. Revised ed. New York, NY: Chelsea House
    Publishers, 2003.

Fisher, Leonard Everett. *Gods and Goddesses of the Ancient Norse*.
    New York, NY: Holiday House, 2001.

Jones, Diana Wynne. *Eight Days of Luke*. New York, NY:
    HarperTrophy, 2003.

Mercatante, Anthony S. *The Facts on File Encyclopedia of World
    Mythology*. New York, NY: Facts on File, 1988.

BIBLIOGRAPHY

Branston, Brian. *Gods of the North*. New York, NY: Thames and Hudson Inc., 1980.

Crossley-Holland, Kevin. *The Norse Myths*. New York, NY: Pantheon Books, 1980.

Davidson, Hilda R. Ellis. *Gods and Myths of Northern Europe*. Baltimore, MD: Pelican Books, 1969.

Davidson, Hilda R. Ellis. *The Lost Beliefs of Northern Europe*. New York, NY: Routledge, 1993.

Davidson, Hilda R. Ellis. *Scandinavian Mythology*. New York, NY: Peter Bedrick Books, 1982.

Hamilton, Edith. *Mythology*. New York, NY: Little, Brown and Company, 1998.

Lindow, John. *Norse Mythology: A Guide to the Gods, Heroes, Rituals, and Beliefs*. New York, NY: Oxford University Press, 2002.

INDEX

About the Author

Jason Porterfield has written numerous nonfiction works for young adults, including a book on Sweden. He also has written about the mythologies of other countries, such as Chile, Argentina, and Vietnam. He earned his B.A. degree from Oberlin College, majoring in English, history, and religion. He lives in Chicago, Illinois.

Photo Credits

Designer: Tom Forget; **Editor:** Joann Jovinelly
Photo Researcher: Amy Feinberg